MW01289803

Emily Gerard & Agnes Murgoci
TRANSYLVANIAN
SUPERSTITIONS

ISBN: 1484196120
ISBN-13: 978-1484196120

Emily Gerard & Agnes Murgoci

Transylvanian Superstitions

SCRIPTA
MINORA
MMXIII

Contents

TRANSYLVANIAN SUPERSTITIONS

Emily Gerard

Transylvania might well be termed the land of superstition, for nowhere else does this curious crooked plant of delusion flourish as persistently and in such bewildering variety. It would almost seem as though the whole species of demons, pixies, witches, and hobgoblins, driven from the rest of Europe by the wand of science, had taken refuge within this mountain rampart, well aware that here they would find secure lurking-places, whence they might defy their persecutors yet awhile.

There are many reasons why these fabulous beings should retain an abnormally firm hold on the soil of these parts; and looking at the matter closely we find here no less than three separate sources of superstition.

First, there is what may be called the indigenous superstition of the country, the scenery of which is peculiarly adapted to serve as background to all sorts of supernatural beings and monsters. There are innumerable caverns, whose mysterious depths seem made to harbour whole legions of evil spirits: forest glades fit only for fairy folk on moonlight nights, solitary lakes which instinctively call up visions of water sprites; golden treasures lying hidden in mountain chasms, all of which have gradually insinuated themselves into the minds of the oldest inhabitants, the Roumenians, and influenced their way of thinking, so that these people, by nature imaginative and poetically inclined, have built up for themselves out of the surrounding materials a whole code of fanciful superstition, to which they adhere as closely as to their religion itself.

Secondly, there is here the imported superstition : that is to say, the old German customs and beliefs brought hither seven hundred years ago by the Saxon colonists from their native land, and like many other things, preserved here in greater perfection than in the original country.

Thirdly, there is the wandering superstition of the gypsy tribes, themselves a race of fortune-tellers and witches, whose ambulating caravans cover the country as with a network, and whose less vagrant members fill up the suburbs of towns and villages.

Of course all these various sorts of superstition have twined and intermingled, acted and reacted upon each other, until in many cases It is a difficult matter to determine the exact parentage of some particular belief or custom; but in a general way the three sources I have named may be admitted as a rough sort of classification in dealing with the principal superstitions afloat in Transylvania.

There is on this subject no truer saying than that of Grimm, to the effect that "superstition in all its manifold varieties constitutes a sort of religion, applicable to the common household necessities of daily life,"[1] and as such, particular forms of superstition may very well

---

[1] "Der Aberglaube in seiner Mannigfaltigkeit bildet gewissermassen eine Religion für den ganzen niederen Hausbedarf."

serve as guide to the characters and habits of the particular nation in which they are prevalent.

The spirit of evil (or, not to put too fine a point upon it, the devil) plays a conspicuous part in the Roumenian code of superstition, and such designations as the *Gregynia Drakuluj* (devil's garden), the *Gania Drakuluj* (devil's mountain), *Yadu Drakuluj* (devil's hell or abyss), &c. &c., which we frequently find attached to rocks, caverns, or heights, attest the fact that these people believe themselves to be surrounded on all sides by a whole legion of evil spirits.

The devils are furthermore assisted by witches and dragons, and to all of these dangerous beings are ascribed peculiar powers on particular days and at certain places. Many and curious are therefore the means by which the Roumenians endeavour to counteract these baleful influences, and a whole complicated study, about as laborious as the mastering of any unknown language, is required in order to teach an unfortunate peasant to steer clear of the dangers by which he considers himself to be beset on all sides. The bringing up of a common domestic cow is apparently as difficult a task as the rearing of any dear gazelle, and even the well-doing of a simple turnip or potato about as precarious as that of the most tender exotic plant.

Of the seven days of the week, Wednesday (*Miercuri*) and Friday (*Vinire*) are considered suspicious days, on which it is not allowed to use needle or scissors, or to bake bread; neither is it wise to sow flax on these days. Venus (called here *Paraschiva*), to whom the Friday is sacred, punishes all infractions of this rule by causing fires or other misfortunes.

Tuesday, however (*Marti*, named from Mars, the bloody god of war), is a decidedly unlucky day, on which spinning is totally prohibited, and even such seemingly harmless pursuits as washing the hands or combing the hair are not unattended by danger. On Tuesday evening about sunset, the evil spirit of that day is in its fullest force, and in many districts the people refrain from leaving their huts between sunset and midnight. "May the *mar sara* (spirit of Tuesday evening) carry you off," is here equivalent to saying "May the devil take you!"

It must not, however, be supposed that Monday, Thursday, and Saturday are unconditionally lucky days, on which the Roumenian is at liberty to do as he pleases. Thus every well educated Roumenian matron knows that she may wash on Thursdays and spin on Saturdays, but that it would be a fatal mistake to reverse the order of these proceedings; and though Thursday is a lucky day for marriage,[2] and is on that account mostly chosen for weddings, it is proportionately unfavourable to agriculture. In many parishes it is considered dangerous to work in the fields on all Thursdays between Easter and Pentecost, and it is believed that if these days are not set aside as days of rest, ravaging hailstorms will be the inevitable punishment of the impiety. Many of the more enlightened Roumenian pastors have preached in vain against this belief, and some years ago the members of a parish presented an official complaint to the bishop, requesting the re-

---

[2] This would seem to suggest a German (or Celtic) origin. Donar, as god of marriages, blesses unions with his hammer.

moval of their *curé*, on the ground that not only he gave bad example by working on the prohibited days, but had actually caused them serious material damage, by the hailstorms his sinful behaviour had provoked.

This respect of the Thursday seems to be the remains of a deeply ingrained, though now unconscious, worship of Jupiter (Zoi), who gives his name to the day.

To different hours of the day are likewise ascribed different influences, favourable or the reverse. Thus it is always considered unlucky to look at oneself in the glass after sunset; also it is not wise to sweep the dust over the threshold in the evening, or to give back a sieve or a whip which has been borrowed of a neighbour.

The exact hour of noon is precarious on account of the evil spirit *Pripolniza*,[3] and so is midnight because of the *miase nópte* (night spirit), and it is safer to remain within doors at these hours. If, however, some misguided peasant does happen to leave his home at midnight, and espies (as very likely he may) a flaming dragon in the sky, he need not necessarily give himself up as lost, for if he have the presence of mind to stick a fork into the ground alongside of him, the fiery monster will thereby be prevented from carrying him off.

The finger which ventures to point at a rainbow will be straightway seized by a gnawing disease, and a

---

[3] This spirit corresponds to the Polednice of the Bohemians and the Poludnica of the Poles and Russians. Grimm, in speaking of the Russians, in his German Mythology, quotes from Boxhorn's *Resp. Moscov.*: "Dæmonemn meridianum Moscovitæ et colunt."

rainbow appearing in December is always considered to bode misfortune.

The Greek Church, to which the Roumenians exclusively belong, has an abnormal number of feast-days, to almost each of which peculiar customs and superstitions are attached. I will here only attempt to mention a few of the principal ones.

On New Year's Day it is customary for the Roumenian to interrogate his fate, by placing a leaf of evergreen on the freshly swept and heated hearthstone. If the leaf takes a gyratory movement he will be lucky, but if it shrivels up where it lies, then he may expect misfortune during the coming year. To ensure the welfare of the cattle it is advisable to place a gold or silver piece in the water-trough, out of which they drink for the first time on New Year's morning.

The feast of the Epiphany or Three Kings (*Tre crai*) is one of the oldest festivals, and was solemnised by the Oriental Church as early as the second century, fully 200 years before it was adopted by the Latins. On this day, which popular belief regards as the coldest in the winter, the blessing of the waters, known as the feast of the Jordan, or *bobetasu* (baptism) feast, takes place. The priests, attired in their richest vestments, proceed to the shore of the nearest river or lake, and bless the waters, which have been unclosed by cutting a Greek cross some six or eight feet long in the surface of the ice. Every pious Roumenian is careful to fill a bottle with the consecrated water before the surface freezes over, and preserves it, tightly corked and sealed up, as an infallible remedy in case of illness.

Particularly lucky is considered whoever dies on that day, for he will be sure to go straight to heaven, the door of which is supposed to stand open all day, in memory of the descent of the Holy Ghost at the baptism of Christ.

The feast of St Theodore, 11th of January (corresponding to our 23rd of January), is a day of rest for the girls, and whichever of them transgresses the rule is liable to be carried off by the saint, who sometimes appears in the shape of a beautiful youth, sometimes as a terrible monster.

The Wednesday in Holy Week is very important. The Easter cakes and breads are baked on this day, and some crumbs are mixed up with the cow's fodder; woe to the woman who indulges in a nap to-day, for the whole year she will not be able to shake off her drowsiness. In the evening the young men in each home bind as many wreaths as there are members of the family: each of these is marked with the name of an individual and thrown up upon the roof. The wreaths which fall down to the ground indicate those who will die that year.

Skin diseases are cured by taking a bath on Good Friday, in a stream or river which flows towards the east.

In the night preceding Easter Sunday witches and demons are abroad, and hidden treasures are said to betray their site by a glowing flame. No God-fearing peasant will, however, allow himself to be tempted by the hopes of such riches, which he cannot on that day appropriate without sin. On no account should he presume to absent himself from the midnight church service, and his devotion will be rewarded by the mystic qualities attached to the wax candle he has carried in his hand, and which when lighted hereafter during a thunderstorm will infallibly keep the lightning from striking his house.

The greatest luck which can befall a mortal is to be born on Easter Sunday while the bells are ringing, but it is not lucky to die on that day. The spoon with which the Easter eggs have been removed from the boiling pot is carefully treasured up, and worn in the belt by the shepherd; it gives him the power to distinguish the witches who seek to molest his flock.

Perhaps the most important day in the year is St. George's, the 23rd of April (corresponds to our 5th of May), the eve of which is still frequently kept by occult meetings taking place at night in lonely caverns or within ruined walls, and where all the ceremonies usual to the celebration of a witches' Sabbath are put into practice.

The feast itself is the great day to beware of witches, to counteract whose influence square-cut blocks of green turf are placed in front of each door and window.[4] This is supposed effectually to bar their entrance to the house or stables, but for still greater safety it is usual here for the peasants to keep watch all night by the sleeping cattle.

This same night is the best for finding treasures, and many people spend it in wandering about the hills trying to probe the earth for the gold it contains. Vain and futile as such researches usually are, yet they have

---

[4] This is also usual in Poland, Moldavia, and the Bukowinq.

in this country a somewhat greater semblance of reason than in most other parts, for perhaps nowhere else have so many successive nations been forced to secrete their riches in flying from an enemy, to say nothing of the numerous veins of undiscovered gold and silver which must be seaming the country in all directions. Not a year passes without bringing to light some earthern jar containing old Dacian coins, or golden ornaments of Roman origin, and all such discoveries serve to feed and keep up the national superstition.

In the night of St. George's Day (so say the legends) all these treasures begin to burn, or, to speak in mystic language, to "bloom" in the bosom of the earth, and the light they give forth, described as a bluish flame resembling the colour of lighted spirits of wine, serves to guide favoured mortals to their place of concealment. The conditions to the successful raising of such a treasure are manifold, and difficult of accomplishment. In the first place, it is by no means easy for a common mortal who has not been born on a Sunday nor at midday when the bells are ringing, to hit upon a treasure at all. If he does, however, catch sight of a flame such as I have described, he must quickly stick a knife through the swaddling rags of his right foot,[5] and then throw the knife in the direction of the flame he has seen. If two people are together during this discovery they must not on any account break silence till the treasure is removed, neither is it allowed to fill up the

---

[5] The Roumenian peasant does not wear shoes or stockings, but has his feet swaddled up in linen rags, which are kept in their place by a rough sandal made of a flat piece of leather.

hole from which anything has been taken, for that would induce a speedy death. Another important feature to be noted is that the lights seen before midnight on St. George's Day denote treasures kept by benevolent spirits, while those which appear at a later hour are unquestionably of a pernicious nature.

For the comfort of less-favoured mortals, who happen neither to have been born on a Sunday, nor during bell-ringing, I must here mention that these deficiencies may be to some extent condoned and the mental vision sharpened by the consumption of mouldy bread; so that whoever has during the preceding year been careful to feed upon decayed loaves only, may (if he survives this trying *régime*) be likewise the fortunate discoverer of hidden treasures.

Sometimes the power of discovering a particular treasure is supposed to be possessed only by members of some particular family. A curious instance of this was lately recorded in Roumenia relating to an old ruined convent, where, according to a popular legend, a large sum of gold is concealed. A deputation of peasants, at considerable trouble and expense, found out the last surviving member of the family supposed to possess the mystic power, and offered him, unconditionally, a very handsome sum merely for his assistance in the search. The gentleman in question, being old, and probably sceptical, declined the offer, to the great disappointment of the peasant deputation.

The feast of St. George, being the day when flocks are first driven out to pasture, is in a special manner the feast of all shepherds and cowherds and on this day only it is allowed to count the flocks and assure oneself of the exact number of sheep. In general, these numbers are but approximately guessed at, and vaguely designated. Thus the Roumenian shepherd, interrogated as to the number of his master's sheep, will probably inform you that they are as numerous as the stars of heaven, or as the daisies which dot the meadows.

The throwing up of wreaths on to the roofs, described above, is in some districts practised on the feast of St. John the Baptist, the 24th of June (July 6th), instead of on the Wednesday in Holy Week. Fires lighted on the mountains this same night are supposed to protect the flocks from evil spirits.

The feast of St. Elias, the 20th of July (August 1), is a very unlucky day, on which the lightning may be expected to strike.

If a house struck by lightning begins to burn, it is not allowed to put out the flames, because God has lit the fire and it would be presumption if man were to dare to meddle.[6] In some places it is believed that a fire lit by lightning can only be put out with milk.

An approved method for averting the danger of the dwelling being struck by lightning is to form a top by sticking a knife through a piece of bread, and spin it on the floor of the loft during the whole time the storm lasts. The ringing of bells is likewise very efficacious, provided, however, that the bell in question has been cast under a perfectly cloudless sky.

As I am on the subject of thunderstorms, I may as well here mention the *Scholomance*, or school supposed to exist somewhere in the heart of the mountains, and

---

[6] Also believed in Poland.

where all the secrets of nature, the language of animals, and all imaginable magic spells and charms are taught by the devil in person. Only ten scholars are admitted at a time, and when the course of learning has expired and nine of them are released to return to their homes; the tenth scholar is detained by the devil as payment, and mounted upon an *Ismeju* (dragon) he becomes henceforward the devil's aide-de-camp, and assists him in "making the weather," that is to say, preparing the thunderbolts.

A small lake, immeasurably deep, lying high up among the mountains to the south of Hermanstadt, is supposed to be the cauldron where is brewed the thunder, and in fair weather the dragon sleeps beneath the waters. Roumenian peasants anxiously warn the traveller to beware of throwing a stone into this lake lest it should wake the dragon and provoke a thunderstorm. It is, however, no mere superstition that in summer there occur almost daily thunderstorms at this spot, about the hour of midday, and numerous cairns of stones round the shores attest the fact that many people have here found their death by lightning. On this account the place is shunned, and no Roumenians will venture to rest here at the hour of noon.

Whoever turns three somersaults the first time he hears the thunder will be free from pains in the back during a twelvemonth, and the man who wishes to be ensured against headache has only to rub it against a stone or knock it with a piece of iron.

The Polish harvest custom of decking out a girl with a wreath of corn ears, and leading her in procession to the house of the landed proprietor, is likewise practised here, with the difference that instead of the songs customary in Poland, the girl is here followed with loud cries of "Prihu! Prihu!" or else "Priku!"[7] and that whoever meets her on the way is bound to sprinkle the wreath with water. If this detail be neglected the next year's crops will assuredly fail. It is also customary to keep the wreaths till next sowing time, when the corn is shaken out, and mingled with the grain to be sowed will ensure a rich harvest.

The feast of St. Spiridion, the 12th of December (corresponding to our 24th), is an ominous day, especially for housewives, and the saint often destroys those who desecrate his feast by manual labour.

That the cattle are endowed with speech during the Christmas night is a general belief, but it is not considered wise to pry upon them and try to overhear what they say, or the listener will rarely overhear any good.

This night is likewise favourable to the discovery of bidden treasures, and the man who has courage to conjure up the evil spirit will be sure to see him if he call upon him at midnight. Three burning coals placed upon the threshold will prevent the devil from carrying him off.

Christmas carols and dramas are also usual among the Roumenians, under the name of Kolinda, supposed to be derived from Kolinda or Lada, goddess of

---

[7]   Archaeologists have derived this word from *Pri*, which in Sanscrit means fruitful, and *Hu*, the god of the Celtic deluge tradition, also regarded as a personification of fruitful nature.

peace.[8] Amongst the parts enacted in these games, are those of Judas, who stands at the door and receives the money collected, and that of the bull, called Turka or Tur,[9] a sort of vague monster fantastically dressed up, half bull, half bear, with a clattering wooden bill, and a dash of Herod about his character, in so far as he is supposed to devour little children, and requires to be propitiated by a copper coin thrust into his bill.[10] In many districts the personating of these characters is supposed to entail a certain amount of odium upon the actors, who are regarded as unclean or bewitched by the devil during a period of six weeks, and may not enter a church nor approach a sacrament till this time has elapsed.

A leaf of evergreen laid into a plate of water on the last day of the year when the bells are ringing will denote health, sickness, or death, during the coming year, according as it is found to be green, spotted, or black on the following morning.

The girl whose thoughts are turned towards love and matrimony has many approved methods of testing her fate on this night.

First of all she may, by cracking the joints of her fingers, accurately ascertain the number of her admirers, also a freshly laid egg broken into a glass of water

---

[8] The Council of Constantinople, 869 A.D., forbade the members of the Oriental Church to keep the feast of the Pagan goddess, Kolinda, occurring on the shortest day.

[9] Called Turon by the Poles, who have many similar games.

[10] This detail would seem to bear some resemblance to Saturn devouring his children, and being cheated by stones thrown into his jaws.

will give much clue to the events in store for her by the shape it adopts. To form a conjecture as to the shape and build of her future husband, she is recommended to throw an armful of firewood as far as she can from her; the piece which has gone furthest will be the image of her intended, according as the stick happens to be tall or short, broad or slender, straight or crooked. If these general indications do not suffice, and she wishes to see the reflection of his face in the water, she has only to step naked at midnight into the nearest lake or river. Very efficacious is it likewise to stand at midnight on the dunghill with a piece of Christmas cake in her mouth, and listen for the first sound of a dog's harking which reaches her ear. From whichever side it proceeds will also come the expected suitor.

Of the household animals, the sheep is the most highly prized by the Roumenian, who makes of it his companion, and frequently his counsellor, and by its bearing it is supposed often to give warning when danger is near.

The swallow is here, as elsewhere, a luck-bringing bird, and goes by the name of *galinele lui Dieu* (fowls of the Lord). There is always a treasure to be found near the place where the first swallow has been espied.

The crow, on the contrary, is a bird of evil omen, and is particularly ominous when it flies straight over the head of any man.[11]

The magpie perched upon a roof gives notice of the approach of guests,[12] but a shrieking magpie meeting or accompanying a traveler denotes death.

---

[11] Likewise in Bavaria.

The cuckoo is an oracle to be consulted in manifold contingencies. This bird plays a great part in Roumenian poetry, and is frequently supposed to be the spirit of an unfortunate lover.

It is never permissible to kill a spider, as that would entail misfortune.

A toad taking up its residence in a cow-byre is assuredly in the service of a witch, and has been sent there to purloin the milk. It should therefore be stoned to death; but the same liberty must not be taken with the equally pernicious weasel, and if these animals be found to inhabit a barn or stable, the peasant must endeavour to render them harmless by diverting their thoughts into a safer channel. To this end a tiny threshing-flail must be prepared for the male weasel, and a distaff for his female partner, and laid at a place the animals are known to frequent.

The skull of a horse placed over the gate of the courtyard,[13] or the bones of fallen animals, buried under the doorstep, are preservatives against ghosts.

The place where a horse has rolled on the ground is unwholesome, and the man who steps upon it will be speedily attacked by eruptions, boils, or other skin diseases.

Black fowls are always viewed with suspicion, as possibly standing in the service of a witch, and the

---

[12] Also believed by most Slav nations.

[13] The original signification of this seems to have gone astray, but was probably based on former worship of the horse, long regarded as a sacred animal by Indians, Parsees, Arabs, and Germans.

Brahmaputra fowl is curiously enough considered to be the offspring of the devil with a Jewish girl.

If a cow has gone astray it will assuredly be eaten by the wolf, unless the owner remembers to stick a pair of scissors in the centre rafter of the dwelling-room.

As a matter of course, such places as churchyards, gallow-trees, and cross-roads are to be avoided, but even the left bank of a river may under circumstances become equally dangerous.

A whirlwind always denotes that the devil is dancing with a witch, and whoever approaches too near to this dangerous circle may be carried off bodily, or at the very least will lose his head-covering.

But the Roumenian does not always endeavour to keep the evil one at arm's length; sometimes, on the contrary, he invokes the devil's assistance, and enters into a regular compact with him.

Supposing, for instance, that he wishes to ensure a flock, garden or field against thieves, wild beasts, or bad weather, the matter is very simple. He has only to repair to a cross-road, at the junction of which he takes up his stand, in the centre of a circle he has traced on the ground. Here, after depositing a copper coin as payment, he summons the demon with the following words:

"Satan, I give thee over my flock (garden or field) to keep till—(such and such a term), that thou mayest defend and protect it for me, and be my servant till this time has expired—"

He must, however, be careful to keep within the circle he has traced, until the devil, who may very likely have chosen to appear in the shape of a goat, crow, toad, or serpent, has completely disappeared, otherwise the unfortunate wretch is irretrievably lost. He is equally sure to lose his soul if he die before the time of the contract has elapsed.

An apothecary of this town (Hermanstadt) told me that he was frequently applied to for a magic potion called *spiridusch*, which is said to have the property of disclosing hidden treasures to its lucky possessor. Only a few weeks ago he received the following letter, published in one of the local papers, and which I have here translated as literally as possible.

> Worthy Sir,—I wish to ask you of something I have been told by others—that is, that you have got for sale a thing they call *spiridusch*, but which, to speak more plainly, is the devil himself. And if this be true, I beg you to tell me if it be really true, and how much it costs; for my poverty is so great and has brought me so far that I must ask the devil to help me. Those who told me this were weak, silly fellows, and were afraid, but I have no fear and have seen many things in my life before; therefore I beg you to write me this, and to take the greeting of an unknown man.— N. N.

Here, as elsewhere, thirteen is an ominous number.

It is unfortunate to meet an old woman or a Roumenian Pope; the meeting of a Protestant or Catholic clergyman is indifferent, and brings neither good nor evil.

It is bad luck if your path be traversed by a hare, but a fox or wolf crossing your road is a good omen.

Likewise, it is lucky to meet a woman with a jug full of water, while an empty jug is unlucky; therefore, the Roumenian maiden who meets you on the way back from the well will, smiling, display her brimming pitcher as she passes, with a pleased consciousness of bringing good luck; while the girl whose pitcher is empty will slink past shamefacedly, as though she had a crime to conceal.

Every orthodox Roumenian woman is careful to do homage to the water-spirit, the *wodna zena* or *zona*, which resides in each spring, by spilling a few drops on the ground, after she has emptied her jug. She will never venture to draw the water against the current, for that would strike the spirit home and provoke her anger.

The Roumenian in general avoids the neighbour-hood of deep pools of water, especially whirlpools, for here resides the dreadful *balaur*, or the *wodna muz*, the cruel waterman who lies in wait for human victims.

Each forest has likewise its own particular spirit, its mama *padura*,[14] or forest mother. This fairy is in general supposed to be good-natured, especially towards children who have lost their way in the wood. Less to be trusted is *Panusch* (surely a corruption of the Greek god Pan?), who haunts the forest glades and lies in wait for helpless maidens.

Ravaging diseases, like the pest, cholera, &c., are at-tributed to a spirit called the *dschuma*, to whom sometimes given the shape of a fierce virgin, sometimes that of a toothless old hag. This spectre can only be

---

[14] So in India the Matris, also known amongst the Egyptians, Chal-deans, and Mexicans. A corresponding spirit is likewise found in the Scandinavian and Lithuanian mythologies; in the latter under the name of *medziajna*.

driven away if a red shirt, which must be spun, woven, and sewed all in one night by seven old women, is hung out at the entrance of the afflicted village.[15]

The body of a drowned man can only be found again by sticking a lighted candle into a hollowed-out loaf of bread and setting it afloat at night on the river or lake. There where the light comes to a standstill will the corpse be found. Until this has been done the water will continue to rise and the rain to fall.

At the birth of a child each one present takes a stone, and throws it behind him, saying, "This into the jaws of the Strigoi," which custom would also seem to suggest Saturn and the swaddled-up stones. As long as the child is unbaptised, it must be carefully watched over, for fear of being changed or otherwise harmed by a witch. A piece of iron or a broom laid under its pillow will keep evil charms away.

Even the Roumenian's wedding day is darkened by the shade of superstition. He can never be quite sure of his affection for his bride being a natural, spontaneous feeling, since it may or will have been caused by the evil influence of a witch. Also at church, when the priest offers the blest bread to himself and his new-made wife, he will tremblingly compare the relative sizes of the two pieces, for whoever chances to get the smaller one must inevitably be the first to die.

But nowhere does the inherent superstition of the Roumenian peasant find stronger expression than in his mourning and funeral ceremonies, which are based upon a totally original conception of death.

---

[15] Also practised in Poland.

Among the various omens of approaching death are the ungrounded barking of a dog or the crowing of a black hen. The influence of the latter may, however, be annulled and the catastrophe averted if the bird be put in a sack and carried thrice round the house.

Boots dug up from the churchyard on Good Friday are to be given to people in danger of death. If, however, this and other remedies fail to save the doomed man, then he must have a burning candle put into his hand; for it is considered to be the greatest of all misfortunes if a man die without a candle—a favour the Roumenian durst not refuse to his most deadly enemy.

The corpse must be washed immediately after death, and the dirt, if necessary, scraped off with knives, because the dead man is more likely to find favour with God if he appears before Him in a clean state. Then he is attired in his best clothes, in doing which great care must be taken not to tie anything in a knot, for that would disturb his rest; likewise, he must not be allowed to carry away any particle of iron about his dress (such as buttons, boot nails, &c.), for this would assuredly prevent him from reaching Paradise, the road to which is long, and is, moreover, divided off by several tolls or ferries. To enable the soul to pass through these a piece of money must be laid in the hand, under the pillow, or beneath the tongue of the corpse. In the neighbourhood of Fogaras, where the ferries or toll-bars are supposed to amount to twenty-five, the hair of the defunct is divided into as many plaits, and a piece of money secured in each. Likewise, a small provision of needles, pins, thread, &c., are put into the coffin to enable the pilgrim to repair any damage his clothes may receive on the way.

The mourning songs, called *Bocete*, usually performed by paid mourners, are directly addressed to the corpse and sung into his ear on either side. This is the last attempt made by the survivors to wake the dead man to life, by reminding him of all he is leaving, and urging him to make a final effort to arouse his dormant faculties—the thought which underlies all these proceedings being, that the dead man hears and sees all that goes on around him, and that it only requires the determined effort of a strong will in order to restore elasticity to the stiffened limbs, and cause the torpid blood to flow again within the veins.

In many places two openings, corresponding to the ears of the deceased, are cut out in the wood of the coffin to enable him to hear the songs of mourning which are sung on either side of him as he is carried to the grave.

This singing into the ears has passed into a proverb, and when the Roumenian says, *i-a-cantat la wechia* (he has sung into his ears), it is tantamount to saying that prayer and admonition have been used in vain.

The *Pomana*, or funeral feast, is invariably held after the funeral, for much of the peace of the defunct depends upon the strict observance of this ceremony. At this banquet all the favourite dishes of the dead man are served, and each guest receives a cake (*colac*) and a jug (*ulcior*), also a wax candle, in his memory. Similar Pomanas are repeated after a fortnight, six weeks, and on each anniversary for the next seven years; also, whenever the defunct has appeared in dream to any member of the family, this likewise calls for another Pomana; and when these conditions are not exactly complied with, the soul thus neglected is apt to wander complaining about the earth, and cannot find rest. These restless spirits, called Strigoi, are not malicious, but their appearance bodes no good, and may be regarded as omens of sickness or misfortune.

More decidedly evil, however, is the vampire, or nosferatu, in whom every Roumenian peasant believes as firmly as he does in heaven or hell. There are two sorts of vampires—living and dead. The living vampire is in general the illegitimate offspring of two illegitimate persons, but even a flawless pedigree will not ensure anyone against the intrusion of a vampire into his family vault, since every person killed by a nosferatu becomes likewise a vampire after death, and will continue to suck the blood of other innocent people till the spirit has been exorcised, either by opening the grave of the person suspected and driving a stake through the corpse, or firing a pistol shot into the coffin. In very obstinate cases it is further recommended to cut off the head and replace it in the coffin with the mouth filled with garlic, or to extract the heart and burn it, strewing the ashes over the grave.

That such remedies are often resorted to, even in our enlightened days, is a well-attested fact, and there are probably few Roumenian villages where such has not taken place within the memory of the inhabitants.

First cousin to the vampire, the long exploded were-wolf of the Germans is here to be found, lingering yet under the name of the *Prikolitsch*. Sometimes it is a dog instead of a wolf, whose form a man has taken either voluntarily or as penance for his sins. In one of the villages a story is still told (and believed) of such a man, who driving home from church on Sunday with his wife, suddenly felt that the time for his transformation had come. He therefore gave over the reins to her, and stepped aside into the bushes, where, murmuring the mystic formula, he turned three somersaults over a ditch. Soon after this the woman, waiting in vain for her husband, was attacked by a furious dog, which rushed, barking, out of the bushes and succeeded in biting her severely, as well as tearing her dress. When, an hour later, this woman reached home alone she was met by her husband, who advanced smiling to meet her, but between his teeth she caught sight of the shreds of her dress which had been bitten out by the dog, and the horror of the discovery caused her to faint away.

Another man used gravely to assert that for more than five years he had gone about in the form of a wolf, leading on a troop of these animals, until a hunter, in striking off his head, restored him to his natural shape.

A French traveller relates an instance of a harmless botanist who, while collecting herbs on a hillside in a crouching attitude, was observed by some peasants at a distance and taken for a wolf. Before they had time to reach him, however, he had risen to his feet and disclosed himself in the form of a man; but this, in the minds of the Roumenians, who now regarded him as an aggravated case of wolf, was but additional motive for attacking him. They were quite sure that he must be a *Prikolitsch*, for only such could change his shape in such an unaccountable manner, and in another minute they were all in full cry after the wretched victim of science, who might have fared badly indeed, had he not happened to gain a carriage on the high road before his pursuers came up.

We do not require to go far for the explanation of the extraordinary tenacity of life of the were-wolf legend in a country like Transylvania, where real wolves still abound. Every winter here brings fresh proof of the boldness and cunning of these terrible animals, whose attacks on flocks and farms are often conducted with a skill which would do honour to a human intellect. Sometimes a whole village is kept in trepidation for weeks together by some particularly audacious leader of a flock of wolves, to whom the peasants not unnaturally attribute a more than animal nature, and one may safely prophesy that so long as the real wolf continues to haunt the Transylvanian forests, so long will his spectre brother survive in the minds of the inhabitants.

Many ancient Roumenian legends tell us that every new church or otherwise important building became a human grave, as it was thought indispensable to its stability to wall in a living man or woman, whose spirit henceforward haunts the place. In later times people having become less cruel, or more probably, because murder is now attended with greater inconvenience to the actors, this custom underwent some modifications, and it became usual in place of a living man to wall in his shadow instead. This is done by measuring the shadow of a person with a long piece of cord, or a ribbon made of strips of reed, and interring this measure instead of the person himself, who, unconscious victim of the spell thrown upon him will pine away and die

31

within forty days. It is an indispensable condition to the success of this proceeding that the chosen victim be ignorant of the part he is playing, therefore careless passers-by near a building place may often hear the warning cry "Beware, lest they take thy shadow!" So deeply engrained is this superstition that not long ago there were still professional shadow-traders, who made it their business to provide architects with the necessary victims for securing their walls. "Of course the man whose shadow is thus interred must die," argues the Roumenian, "but as he is unaware of his doom he does not feel any pain or anxiety, so it is less cruel than walling in a living man."

The superstitions afloat among the Saxon peasantry of Transylvania relate oftenest to household matters, such as the well-being of cattle and poultry and the success of the harvest or vintage. There is more of the quack, and less of the romantic element to be found here, and the invisible spiritual world plays less part in their beliefs. Some of the most prevalent Saxon superstitions are as follows:

1. Whoever can blow back the flame into a candle which has just been extinguished will become pastor.

2. In going into a new-built house one must throw in a dog or a cat before entering, otherwise one of the family will soon die.

3. If a swallow fly under a cow straightway the milk will become bloody.

4. Whoever enters a strange house should sit down, were it only for a second, otherwise he will deprive the inhabitants of their sleep.

5. Whoever has been robbed of anything and wants to discover the thief, must select a black hen, and for nine consecutive Fridays must, as well as the hen, abstain from all food. The thief will then either die or bring back the stolen goods. (This is called taking up the black fast against a person.)

6. It is not good to point with the finger at an approaching thunderstorm; likewise, whoever stands over-long gazing at the summer lightning will go mad.

7. A person ill with the fever should be covered up with nine articles of clothing, each of a different colour and material: he will then recover.

8. Another way to get rid of the fever is to go into an inn or public-house, and after having drunk a glass of wine to go out again without speaking or paying, but leaving behind some article of clothing which is of greater value than the wine drunk.

9. Drinking out of seven different wells is likewise good for the fever.

10. Or else go into the garden when no one is looking, shake a young fruit tree and return to the house without looking back; the fever will then have passed into the tree.

11. Any article purposely dropped on the ground when out walking will convey the fever to whoever finds it. This method is, however, to be distrusted (we are told by village authorities), for the finder may avert the illness by thrice spitting on the thing in question. Spitting on all and every occasion is in general very efficacious for averting spells and other evils.

12. A hailstorm may sometimes be stopped by a knife stuck into the ground in front of the house.

13. A new servant must be allowed to eat freely the first day he or she enters service, otherwise their hunger will never be stilled.

14. It is bad luck to rock an empty cradle.

15. When someone has just died the window must be opened to let the soul escape.

16. It is not considered good to count the beehives or the loaves when they are put into the oven.

17. When the master of the house dies, one must go and tell it to the bees, and to the cattle in the stables, otherwise some new misfortune is sure to happen.

18. If the New Year's night be clear the hens will lay many eggs during the year.

19. It is not good to whitewash the house when the moon is decreasing, for that produces bugs.

20. Who eats mouldy bread will be rich and longlived.

21. Subbing the body with garlic is a preservative against witchcraft and the pest.

22. Licking the platter clean at table will bring fine weather.

23. A funeral at which the bells are not rung brings hail.

24. When foxes and wolves meet in the market-place then prices will rise (naturally, since wolves and foxes could only be so bold during the greatest cold, when prices of eggs, butter, &c., are always at their highest).

25. To keep sparrows off a field or garden it is only necessary to sprinkle earth taken at midnight from the churchyard over the place.

26. A broom put upside down behind the door will keep away the witches.

27. It is bad luck to lay a loaf upside down on the table.

28. In carrying a child to church to be christened it is important to carry it by the broadest streets, and to avoid narrow lanes and byways, else when it is big it will become a thief.

29. If a murderer be confronted with the corpse of his victim the wounds will begin to bleed again.[16]

30. Avoid a toad, as it may be a witch.

31. Little children's nails should be bitten off instead of out the first time, lest they learn to steal.

32. An approved sort of love charm is to take the two hind legs of a green tree-frog, bury these in an ant-hill till all the flesh is removed, then tie them up securely in a linen handkerchief, and whosoever touches this linen will be seized at once with love for its owner.

33. To avert many illnesses which may occur to the pigs, it is still customary in some places for the swineherd to dispense with his clothes the first time he drives out his pigs to pasture in spring. A newly elected clergyman, regarding this practice as immoral, tried to forbid it in his parish, but was sternly asked by the village, bailiff whether he was prepared to pay for all the pigs which would assuredly die that year in consequence of the omission.

34. The same absence of costume is likewise recommended to women assisting a cow to calve.

The night of St. Thomas (21st of December) is the date consecrated by Saxon superstition to the celebration of the games which elsewhere are usual on All-

---

[16] Also believed by the Roumenians.

Halloween. Every girl puts her fate to the test on this evening, and there are various ways of so doing (too lengthy to be here described), with shoes, flowers, onions, &c. For the twelve days following it is not allowed to spin, and the young men who visit the spinning-room of the girls have the right to break and burn all the distaffs they find, so it has become usual for the maidens to appear with a stick dressed up with wool to represent the distaff instead of a real spinning-wheel.

Some of the Saxon customs are peculiarly interesting from being obviously remnants of Paganism, and are a curious proof of the force of verbal tradition, which in this case has not only borne the transplantation from a far distant country, but likewise weathered the storm of two successive changes of religion.

A very strong proof of the tenacity of Pagan habits and train of thought is, I think, the fact, that although at the time these Saxon colonists appeared in Transylvania, towards the second part of the twelfth century, they had already belonged to the Christian Church for more than three hundred years, yet many points of the landscape in their new home baptized by them have received Pagan appellations. Thus we find the *Götzenberg*,[17] or mountain of the gods, and the *wodesch* and the *wolnk* applied to woods and plains, both evidently derived from Wodan.

Many old Pagan ceremonies are still clearly to be distinguished through the flimsy shrouding of a later period, and their origin unmistakable even through the surface-varnish of Christianity which was thought nec-

---

[17] The word *Götzen* in German signifies Pagan deities.

essary to adapt them to newer circumstances, and like a clumsily remodelled garment the original cut frequently asserts itself, despite the fashionable trimmings which now adorn it. In many popular rhymes and dialogues, for instance, it has been clearly proved that those parts now assigned to the Saviour and St. Peter originally belonged to the old gods Thor and Loki; while the faithless Judas has had the personification of a whole hoard of German demons thrust upon him. It is likewise strongly to be suspected that St. Elias who in some parts of Hungary, as well as in Roumenia, Servia, and Croatia, is considered the proper person to be invoked in thunderstorms, is verily no other than the old thunder god Thor, under a Christian mask.

One of the most striking of the Christianised dramas just mentioned is the *Todanstragen*, or throwing out the Death, a custom still extant in several of the Transylvanian Saxon villages, and which may likewise be found still existing in some remote parts of Germany. The feast of the Ascension is the day on which this ceremony takes place in a village of this neighbourhood. It is conducted in the following manner:

After forenoon church on that day, the school-girls of the parish repair to the house of one of their companions, and there proceed to dress up the "Death." This is done by tying up a threshed-out corn-sheaf into the rough semblance of a head and body, while the arms are simulated by a broomstick stuck horizontally. This done, the figure is dressed up in the Sunday clothes of a young village matron, the head adorned with the customary cap and veil fastened by silver pins; two large black beads, or black-headed pins, represent the eyes, and thus equipped the figure is displayed at the open window, in order that all people may see it, on their way to afternoon church. The conclusion of vespers[18] is the signal for the girls to seize the figure and open the procession round the village; two of the eldest girls hold the "Death" between them, and the others follow in regular order two and two, singing a Lutheran Church hymn. The boys are excluded from the procession, and must content themselves with admiring the *Schöner Tod* (handsome Death) from a distance. When all the village streets have been traversed in this manner, the girls repair to another house, whose door is locked against the besieging troop of boys. The figure Death is here stripped of its gaudy attire, and the naked straw bundle thrown out of the window, whereupon it is seized by the boys and carried off in triumph to be thrown into the neighbouring stream or river. This is the first part of the drama, while the second consists in one of the girls being solemnly invested with the clothes and ornaments previously worn by the figure, and like it, led in procession round the village to the singing of the same hymn as before. This is to represent the arrival of summer. The ceremony terminates by a feast given by the parents of the girl who has acted the principal part, from which the boys are again excluded.

---

[18] Afternoon church is always called vespers by the Saxon villager, though I believe it has no resemblance to the chanted vespers of the Roman Catholics.

According to popular belief it is allowed to eat fruits only after this day, as now the "Death," that is, the unwholesomeness, has been expelled from them. Also the river in which the Death has been drowned may now be considered fit for public bathing.

If this ceremony be ever omitted in the villages where it is customary, this neglect is supposed to entail the death of one of the youths or maidens.

This same ceremony may, as I have said, be found still lingering in many other places, everywhere with slight variations. There are villages where the figure is burnt instead of drowned, and Passion Sunday (often called the Dead Sunday), or else the 25th of March, are the days sometimes chosen for its accomplishment. In some places it was usual for the straw figure to be attired in the shirt of the last person who had died, and with the veil of the most recent bride on its head. Also the figure is occasionally pelted with stones by the youth of both sexes; whoever hits it will not die during the year.

At Nuremberg little girls dressed in white used to go in procession through the town, carrying a small open coffin, in which a doll was laid out in state, or sometimes only a stick dressed up, with an apple to represent the head.

In many of these German places, the rhymes which are sung apply to the advent of summer and the extinction of winter, such as the following:—

And now we have chased the death away
And brought in the summer so warm and so gay;
The summer and the month of May

> We bring sweet flowers full many a one.
> We bring the rays of the golden sun,
> For the dreary death at last is gone.

or else,

> Come all of you and do not tarry
> The evil death away to carry;
> Come, spring, once more, with us to dwell,
> Welcome, O spring, in wood and dell!

And there is no doubt that similar rhymes used also to be sung here, until they were replaced by the Lutheran hymns.

Some German archaeologists have attempted to prove that "death" in these games is of more recent introduction, and has replaced the "winter" of former times, so as to give the ceremony a more Christian colouring by the allusion of the triumph of Christ over death, on His resurrection and ascension into heaven. Without presuming to contradict the many well-known authorities who have taken this view of the case, I cannot help thinking that it hardly requires such explanation to account for the presence of death in these dramas. Nowadays, when luxury and civilisation have done so much towards equalising all seasons, so that we can never be deprived of flowers in winter, nor want for ice in summer, we can with difficulty realise the enormous gulf which in olden times separated winter from summer. Not only in winter were all means of communication cut off for a large proportion of people, but their very existence was, so to say, frozen up; and if the granaries were scantily filed, or the in-clement season prolonged by some weeks, death was literally standing at the door of thousands of poor wretches. No wonder, then, that winter and death became identical in their minds, and that they hailed the advent of spring with delirious joy, dancing round the first violet, and following about the first cockchafer in solemn procession. It was the feast of Nature which they celebrated then as now—Nature mighty and eternal—which must always remain essentially the same, whether decked out in Pagan or Christian garb.

Another remnant of Paganism is the *Feurix* or *Feuriswolf* which lingers yet in the mind of these people. According to ancient German mythology the *Feuriswolf* is a monster which, on the last day, is to open his mouth so wide that the top jaw touches the sky, and the lower one the earth; and not long ago a Saxon woman bitterly complained in a court of justice that her husband had cursed her over strongly, in saying, "Der wärlthangd saul dich frieszen;" literally, "May the world-dog swallow thee!"

The gipsies take up a different position as regards superstition from either Roumenian or Saxon, since they may be rather considered to be direct causes and mainsprings of superstition, than victims of credulity themselves. The Tzigane, whose religion is of such an extremely superficial nature that he rarely believes in anything as complicated as the immortality of the soul, can hardly be supposed to lay much weight upon the supernatural; and if he instinctively avoids such places as churchyards, gallow-trees, &c., his feelings are rather those of a child who shirks being reminded of anything so unpleasant as death or burial.

That, however, these people exercise a considerable influence on their Saxon and Roumenian neighbours is undoubted, and it is a paradoxical fact, that the same people who regard the gipsy as an undoubted thief, liar, and cheat, in all the common transactions of daily life, do not hesitate to confide in him blindly for charmed medicines and love-potions, and are ready to attribute to him unerring power in deciphering the mysteries of the future.

The Saxon peasant will, it is true, often drive away the fortuneteller with blows and curses from his door, but his wife, as often as not, will secretly beckon to her to come in again by the back door, in order to be consulted as to the illness of the cows, or to beg from her a remedy against the fever.

Wonderful potions and salves, in which the fat of bears, dogs, snakes and snails, along with the oil of rain-worms, the bodies of spiders and midges rubbed into a paste, and many other similar ingredients, are concocted by these cunning Bohemians, who will sometimes thus make thrice as much money out of the carcass of a dead dog as another from the sale of three healthy pigs.

It has also been averred that both Roumenian and Saxon mothers, whose sickly infants are thought to be suffering from the effects of the evil eye, are frequently in the habit of giving the child to be nursed for a period of nine days to some gipsy woman, who is supposed to be able to undo the spell.

There is not a village which does not boast of one or more fortunetellers, and living in the suburbs of each town are many old women who make an easy and comfortable livelihood only by imposing on the credulity of their fellow-creatures.

The gipsies, one of whose principal trades is the burning of bricks and tiles, are often accused of occasioning lengthy droughts to suit their own purposes. When this has occurred, and the necessary rains have not been produced by soundly beating the guilty Tziganes, the Roumenians sometimes resort to the *Papaluga*, or Rain-maiden. This is done by stripping a young gipsy girl quite naked, and dressing her up with wreaths of flowers and leaves which entirely cover her up, leaving only the head visible. Thus adorned, the Papaluga is conducted round the villages in procession, to the sound of music and singing, and everyone hastens to water her copiously.

If also the Papaluga fails to bring the desired rain, then the evil must evidently be of a deeper and more serious nature, and is to be attributed to a vampire, who must be sought out and destroyed in the manner described above.

The part of the Papaluga is also sometimes enacted by a Roumenian maiden, when there is no reason to suspect the gipsies of being concerned in the drought. This custom of the Rain-maiden is also to be found in Servia, and I believe in Croatia.

It would be endless were I to attempt to enumerate all the different sorts of superstition afloat in this country; for besides the three principal definitions here given, the subject comprises innumerable other side branches, and might further be divided into the folk-lore of shepherds, farmers, hunters, miners, fishermen, &c., each of these separate callings having its own peculiar set of signs, customs, charms, and traditions to go by.

Superstition is an evil which every person with a well-balanced mind should wish to die out, yet it cannot be denied that some of these fancies are graceful and suggestive. Nettles and briars, albeit mischievous plants, may yet come in picturesquely in a landscape; and although the stern agriculturist is bound to rejoice at their uprooting, the softer-hearted artist is surely free to give them a passing sigh of regret.

[*The Nineteenth Century*, vol. 18, London, 1885]

THE VAMPIRE IN ROUMANIA

Agnes Murgoci

The folklore of vampires is of special interest from the light it throws on primitive ideas about body and soul, and about the relation of the body and soul after death.

In Russia, Roumania, and the Balkan states there is an idea—sometimes vague, sometimes fairly definite—that the soul does not finally leave the body and enter into Paradise until forty days after death. It is supposed that it may even linger for years, and when this is the case decomposition is delayed. In Roumania, bodies are disinterred at an interval of three years after death in the case of a child, of four or five years in the case of young folk, and of seven years in the case of elderly people. If decomposition is not then complete, it is supposed that the corpse is a vampire; if it is complete, and the bones are white and clean, it is a sign that the soul has entered into eternal rest. The bones are washed in water and wine and put in clean linen, a religious service is held, and they are reinterred.

In Bukovina and the surrounding districts there was an orgy of burials and reburials in the years 1919 and 1920, for not only were people dying of epidemics and hardships, but also the people who had died in the early years of the war had to be disinterred.

It is now considered to be exceptional that a spirit should reanimate its body and walk as a vampire, but,

45

in a vampire story quoted below, it is said that they were once as common as blades of grass. It would seem that the most primitive phase of the vampire belief was that all departed spirits wished evil to those left, and that special means had to be taken in all cases to prevent their return. The most typical vampire is therefore the reanimated corpse. We may call this the dead-vampire type.

People destined to become vampires after death may be able in life to send out their souls, and even their bodies, to wander at crossroads with reanimated corpses. This type may be called the live-vampire type. It merges into the ordinary witch or wizard, who can meet other witches or wizards either in the body or as a spirit.

A third type of vampire is the *vârcolac*, which eats the sun and moon during eclipses.

A typical vampire of the reanimated-corpse type may have the attributes of a lover, as in Scott's William and Helen. The *zmeu* may also be such a lover.

The *strigele* (sing. *striga*) are not really vampires, but are sometimes confused with them. They are spirits either of living witches, which these send out as a little light, or of dead witches who can find no resting place. These *strigele* come together in uneven numbers, seven or nine. They meet on rocky mountains, and dance and say:

Nup, Cuisnup,
In cas a cu ustoroi nu ma duc.

[Nup, Cuisnup, I won't enter any
house where there is garlic.]

46

They are seen as little points of light floating in the air. Their dances are exquisitely beautiful. Seven or nine lights start in a line, and then form into various figures, ending up in a circle. After they break off their dance, they may do mischief to human beings.

As regards the names used for vampires, dead and alive, *strigoi* (fem. *strigoica*) is the most common Roumanian term, and *moroii* is perhaps the next most usual. *Moroii* is less often used alone than *strigoi*. Usually we have *strigoi* and *moroii* consorting together, but the *moroii* are subject to the *strigoi*. We find also *strigoi*, *moroii*, and *vârcolaci*, and *strigoi* and *pricolici* used as if all were birds of the same feather. A Transilvanian term is *şişcoi*. *Vârcolaci* (*svârcolaci*) and *pricolici* are sometimes dead vampires, and sometimes animals which eat the moon. *Oper* is the Ruthenian word for dead vampire. In Bukovina, *vidme* is used for a witch; it covers much the same ground as *strigoi* (used for a live vampire), but it is never used for a dead vampire. *Diavoloace*, beings with two horns and spurs on their sides and feet, are much the same as *vidme*.

As Dr. Gaster reminds me, in many disenchantments we find phrases such as:

De strigoaica, de strigoi,
Și de case cu moroi.

[From vampires (male and female),
and from a home with vampires.]

De deochetori și de deochetoare,
De moroi, cu moroaiça,
De strigoi cu strigoaica.

[From those who cast the evil eye
(male or female), from vampires
(male and female).]

Ci, íi dracul cu drácoaica, striga cu strigoiul,
Deochiu cu deochitorul, pociturá cu pocitorul,
Potca cu potcoiul.

[The devil with the female devil, the spirit of
the dead witch with the vampire (male), the evil eye
with the caster of the evil eye, the bewitchment with the
bewitcher, the quarrel with the mischief-maker.]

Ciuma, the plague, is occasionally one of the party. The *strigoi* and *moroi* are almost inseparable, hunting, however, with witches, wizards, and devils.

The nature spirits (*ielele* and *dansele*) usually have disenchantments of their own, for they work apart from vampires and wizards, who are beings of human origin. While the peasant groups nature spirits apart from the more human workers of evil, he groups the living and the dead together, for the caster of the evil eye and the bewitcher are living men, though prospective vampires. The vampire, in fact, forms a convenient transition between human workers of evil and the devil, who resembles the dead vampire in not being alive in the flesh.

The vampire (a reanimated corpse) and the devil (a spirit) ought not, strictly speaking, to be alike, but the peasant, finding it difficult to imagine a spirit without a body, thinks of the devil in the form of a crow or a cat, or even in a quasi-human form. The devil is a target for the thunderbolts of St. Elijah, and can be transfixed by one. Even the spirit of a living man, if separated from his body, must have some body or form. In Transilvania it is thought that many people can project their soul as a butterfly. In Vălcea souls of vampires are considered to be incarnated in death's-head moths, which, when caught, should be impaled on a pin and stuck to a wall to prevent their flying further. A small, graceful thing which flutters in the air like a butterfly or a moth is as near as these peasants can get to the idea of pure spirit. The peasant in Siret goes a step further when he conceives of the soul as a little light. He has got beyond what is tangible.

The belief in vampires has often caused trouble to the rulers of Roumania. Ureche, in his History of Roumania, quotes the following:

In 1801, on July the 12th, the Bishop of Siges sends a petition to the ruler of Wallachia, that he should order his rulers of provinces to permit no longer that the peasants of Stroesti should dig up dead people, who had already been dug up twice under the idea that they were vârcolaci [term here used instead of strigoi].

In the *Biserica Orthodoxa Romana* (an 28) there is the following:

The Archbishop Nectarie (1813-19) sent round a circular to his higher clergy (protopopes) exhorting them to find out in what districts it was thought that the dead became vampires. If they came on a case of vampirism they were not to take it upon themselves to burn the corpse, but to teach the people how to proceed according to the written roll of the church.

The following accounts of vampires are taken from the Roumanian periodical of peasant art and literature, *Ion Creanga*. It was edited by my late friend, Tudor Pamfile, one of the most competent and industrious folklorists Roumania has ever had. The stories in *Ion Creanga*were taken down by careful observers, and published as nearly as possible in the exact words of the peasants.

N. I. Dumitrascu is responsible for the following, printed in Ion *Creanga*:[1]

Some twenty or thirty years ago (from 1914) in the commune Afumati in Dolj, a certain peasant, Mărin Mirea Ociocioc, died. It was noticed that his relations also died, one after the other. A certain Badea Vrajitor (Badea the wizard) dug him up. Badea himself, going later into the forest up to the frontier on a cold wintry night, was eaten by wolves. The bones of Mărin were sprinkled with wine, a church service read over them, and replaced in the grave. From that time there were no more deaths in the family.

Some fifteen years ago, in Amărăşti in the north of Dolj, an old woman, the mother of the peasant Dinu Gheorghiţa, died. After some months the children of her eldest son began to die, one after the other, and, after that, the children of her youngest son. The sons became anxious, dug her up one night, cut her in two, and buried her again. Still the deaths did not cease. They dug her up a second time, and what did they see? The body whole without a wound. It was a great marvel. They took her and carried her into the forest, and put her under a great tree in a re-

---

[1] *Ion Creanga,* 7 (1914): 165.

mote part of the forest. There they disembowelled her, took out her heart, from which blood was flowing, cut it in four, put it on hot cinders, and burnt it. They took the ashes and gave them to children to drink with water. They threw the body on the fire, burnt it, and buried the ashes of the body. Then the deaths ceased.

Some twenty or thirty years ago, a cripple, an unmarried man, of Cuşmir, in the south of Mehedinp, died. A little time after, his relations began to die, or to fall ill. They complained that a leg was drying up. This happened in several places. What could it be? "Perhaps it is the cripple; let us dig him up." They dug him up on Saturday night, and found him as red as red, and all drawn up into a corner of the grave. They cut him open, and took the customary measures. They took out the heart and liver, burnt them on red-hot cinders, and gave the ashes to his sister and other relations, who were ill. They drank them with water, and regained their health.

In the Cuşmir, another family began to show very frequent deaths, and suspicion fell on a certain old man, dead long ago. When they dug him up, they found him sitting up like a Turk, and as red as red, just like fire; for had he not eaten up nearly the whole of a family of strong, young men. When they tried to get him out he resisted, unclean and horrible. They gave him some blows with an axe, they got him out, but they could not cut him with a knife. They took a scythe and an axe, cut out his heart and liver, burnt them, and gave them to the sick folk to drink. They drank, and regained their health. The old man was reburied, and the deaths ceased.

In Văguileşti, in Mehedinţi, there was a peasant Dimitriu Vaideanu, of Transilvanian origin, who had married a wife in Văguileşti and settled there. His children died one after the other; seven died within a few months of birth, and some bigger children had died as well. People began to wonder what the cause of all this could be. They took council together, and resolved to take a white horse to the cemetery one night, and see if it would pass over the graves of the wife's relations. This they did, and the horse jumped over all the graves, until it came to the grave of the mother-in-law, Joana Marta, who had been a witch, renowned far and wide. Then the horse stood still, beating the earth with its feet, neighing, and snorting, unable to step over the grave. Probably there was something unholy there. At night Dimitriu and his son took candles and went to dig up the grave. They were seized with horror at what they saw. There she was, sitting like a Turk, with long hair falling over her face, with all her skin red, and with finger nails frightfully long. They got together brushwood, shavings, and bits of old crosses, they poured wine on her, they put in straw, and set fire to the whole. Then they shovelled the earth back and went home.

Slightly different methods are described by other observers as employed in other districts:

In Romanap the vampire was disinterred, undressed, and put in a bag. The clothes were put back into the coffin and sprinkled with holy water, the coffin put back into the grave, and the grave closed. A strong man carried the body to the forest. The heart was cut out, and the body cut up and one piece after another burnt. Last of all the heart was burnt, and those present came near so that the smoke passed over them, and protected them from evil. Here, as elsewhere, it is emphasized that the burning must be complete. If the smallest piece of bone remains unburnt, the vampire can grow up again from it.

In Zârneşti, when the vampire is dug up, iron forks are put into her heart, eyes, and breast, and she is reburied with her face downwards.

In Mehedinţi it is sometimes considered sufficient to take the corpse far away to the mountains and leave it there. This is comparable with, but would not appear to be so efficient as, the Greek plan of taking the body of a vampire over the sea to an island.

The most general method for dealing with a vampire is as follows: It must be exhumed on a Saturday, as on all other days it will be wandering away from the grave. Either put a stake through the navel or take out the heart. The heart may be burnt on charcoal, or in a fire; it may be boiled, or cut into bits with a scythe. If the heart is burnt, the ashes must be collected. Sometimes they are got rid of by throwing into a river, but usually they are mixed with water and given to sick people to drink. They may also be used to anoint children and animals as a means of warding off anything unclean. Sometimes, however, the curse of a priest is sufficient to seal a vampire in its tomb.

The tests to determine whether any dead man is a vampire, or not, are as follows:

1. His household, his family, and his live stock, and possibly even the live stock of the whole village, die off rapidly.

2. He comes back in the night and speaks with the family. He may eat what he finds in dishes and knock things about, or he may help with the housework and cut wood. Female vampires also come back to their children. There was a Hungarian vampire which could not be kept away, even by the priest and holy water.

3. The priest reads a service at the grave. If the evil which is occurring does not cease, it is a bad sign.

4. A hole about the size of a serpent may be found near the tombstone of the dead man. If so, it is a sign of a vampire, because vampires come out of graves by just such holes.

5. Even in the daytime a white horse will not walk over the grave of a vampire, but stands still and snorts and neighs.

6. A gander, similarly, will not walk over the grave of a vampire.

7. On exhuming the corpse, if it is a vampire it will be found to be:
   a) red in the face, even for months and years after burial,
   b) with the face turned downwards,
   c) with a foot retracted and forced into a corner of the grave or coffin.
   d) If relations have died, the mouth will be red with blood. If it has only spoilt and ruined things at home, and eaten what it could find, the mouth will be covered with maize meal.

If the vampire is not recognized as such, and rendered innocuous, it goes on with its evil ways for seven years. First it destroys its relations, then it destroys men and animals in its village and in its country, next it passes into another country, or to where another language is spoken, and becomes a man again. He marries, and has children, and the children, after they die, all become vampires and eat the relations of their mother. As Miss Durham says, this action of a vampire is probably suggested by the epidemics which wipe out families and indeed villages in the countries of southeastern Europe. If, however, we assume a vampire for every epidemic, they would certainly be only less plentiful than leaves of grass.

In case it is feared that any man may become a vampire, precautions must be taken at burial or soon after. As suicides are potential vampires, they should be dug up at once from their graves, and put into running water. A man may know that he was born with a caul, and leave word what is to be done to save his family from disaster. Or his relations may know of the danger and guard against it. There are various methods of avoiding this danger, and several may be used at the same time. The commonest method is to drive a stake through the heart or navel. In Vălcea, it is sufficient to put a needle into the heart, but in Bulgaria it is a red-hot iron which is driven through the heart. Small stones and incense should be put in the mouth, nose, ears, and navel, and under the finger nails, "so that the vampire may have something to gnaw." Garlic may also be placed in the mouth. Millet may be put in the coffin, or in the mouth and nose, so that the vampire will delay many days till it has eaten the millet. The body should be placed face downwards in the coffin. If it is a case of reburial, the corpse should be turned head to foot.

A nail may be put under the tongue. The coffin should be bound with trailers of wild roses, or other bands of wood. In Teleorman, when people go to the house of death on the third day in order to burn incense, they take nine distaffs, which they stick into the grave. If the corpse should rise, it would be pierced by them. They also take tow, strew it on the grave, and set fire to it, so that it shall singe the vampire.

Although in Roumanian folklore vampires and devils are fairly nearly akin, I have found so far no instance in which the dead corpse is supposed to be reanimated by a devil and not by its own soul. This, however, is what is described as happening in Ralston's *Russian Folk Tales*.[2] In Serbia and Bulgaria a nail should be put in the back of the neck, as well as a stake through the heart, so that the devil who means to use the body as a vampire may not be able to distend the skin.

The causes of vampirism are various. Roumanians think that a man born with a caul becomes a vampire within six weeks after his death; similarly people who were bad and had done evil deeds in their lifetime, and more especially women who have had to do with the evil one and with spells and incantations. It is known that a man is a vampire if he does not eat garlic; this idea is also found among the South Slavs. When a child dies before it is baptized, it becomes a vampire at seven years of age, and the place where it was buried is

---

[2]   W. R. S. Ralston, *Russian Folk Tales* (London, 1873),318.

unholy. Men who swear falsely for money become vampires six months after death. If a vampire casts its eye on a pregnant woman, and she is not disenchanted, her child will be a vampire. If a pregnant woman does not eat salt, her child will be a vampire. When there are seven children of the same sex, the seventh will have a little tail and be a vampire. A dead man becomes a vampire, if a cat jumps over him, if a man steps over him, or even if the shadow of a man falls over him. Some Roumanians think that, if people are fated to be vampires, they will become one whether they wish it or not. Then during their lifetime, when they sleep, their soul comes out of their mouth like a little fly. If, during sleep, the body is turned round so that the head is where the feet were before, the man dies.

Other Roumanians think that even if a child is born with a caul, i.e., is born to be a vampire, something can be done to mend matters. In the first place, the caul must be broken at once, so that the child may not swallow it and remain an evil vampire, casting the evil eye all its life, and eating its relations after death. The midwife should go outside with the baby, after it is washed and wrapped up. If it is a dug-out house, half underground, she should go onto the top of it; otherwise she goes to the back, and calls out with the baby in her arms, "Hear, everyone, a wolf is born onto the earth. It is not a wolf that will eat people, but a wolf that will work and bring luck." In this way, the power of the vampire is broken, and evil turns to good. For vampires who are no longer vampires bring luck.

If a dead man, supposed to be a vampire, has a brother born on the same day of the year, or month of the year, as himself, there is great danger of the dead vampire causing the living brother to become a vampire. This must be prevented by a process called "taking out of iron." An iron chain, the one used for hanging the pot over the fire, or one used in bullock carts, is taken and put round the two brothers. The ends are solemnly closed and opened three times, and usually the priest reads a religious service. When the iron is opened for the last time, the living brother is free—he is no longer in danger of becoming a vampire.

There are various characters which distinguish the dead-vampire type only, others common to both types, and a great many which belong to live vampires and witches only. It is said that *strigoi* meet *moroii* and *vârcolaci* at the boundaries, and decide on their program of evil for the coming year—who is to be killed and by whom. Elsewhere it is said that at these same boundaries, where neither the cuckoo sings nor the dog barks, the dead vampires meet the living ones, and teach them all sorts of incantations and spells. They meet also in churchyards, in ruined or deserted houses, or in the forest. They may quarrel among themselves, and fight, using the tongues of hemp brakes,[3] or more rarely

---

[3] The hemp brake used by the Roumanian peasant consists of a narrowish, trestlelike table or stand. At one end an H-axle is fixed. Jointed to this is the tongue, an object like a T -shaped hammer with the horizontal part of the T very flat and broad, and often made of iron. The stalks of the hemp are laid on the table in the direction of its length, and the head of the hammer is brought down on them again and again till they are thoroughly crushed. Sometimes the H-axle of the hemp brake is in the center of the table, and there is a tongue at either end. When this is so, two women can work at their hemp crushing at the same time.

swords, as weapons. Once a man, who was walking round a cemetery, met a vampire, who forced him to carry his hemp brake for him. The man was hardly able to get home, and was ill in bed for many months after. Another man saw a female vampire near a cemetery, and threw a stone at her. She caused an evil wind to blow on him, and it blew him down and took away his senses. He never regained his reason. Apoplexy is also caused by bewitchment by a dead vampire.

Peasants who are thinking of live rather than dead vampires tell us that they walk out to the boundaries of villages, the women together with their head, and the men with their head. They have signs that enable them to bewitch all living things and do what they like with them. Thinking only of live vampires, peasants from Mihalcea and the neighborhood tell us that it is chiefly women who are vampires. One may be specially for hens, another for ducks, and another for lizards. They take the "power" (Roum. *mana*) of these animals for themselves. Some take the milk and "power" of women. Some have special power over bread, others over rain, over hens, or over bees. They take the "power" of bees and bring it to their mistress. If bees lose their "power," they no longer collect honey, and they have nothing to eat even for themselves. There was once a woman who made bread that was so good that half the village ate it. No one else could get such a pleasing taste as she did. This was because she knew how to take the "power" of bread from other women.

It is more especially on St. George's Eve that these vampires go to the boundaries to take rain and the "power" of animals, so as to have enough for the whole year. If they do not take "power" for themselves, they take it for those who pay them. They bring "power" and beauty to women who pay; also they cause men to hate the rivals of those who hire them. They can take "power" from women, and thus take milk away from nursing mothers. They can turn themselves into horses, dogs, or cats, so as to frighten people. The female vampires are dry in the body and are red in the face both before and after death. They go out on St. Andrew's Eve to the boundaries even if they have just borne children. They get out by the chimney, and come back worn out and in rags. The male vampires are bald, and after death grow a tail and hooves.

When a vampire washes itself, rain will fall from heaven. Thus, when a drought occurs, nobles send all their men to wash, because any of them may be a vampire. The moment any vampire wets its tail, there is rain. Vampires never drown, they always float on top. It is usually special vampires (live) who have power over rain; however, heavy rains in Zârneşti were supposed to be caused by a recently buried girl, thought to be a vampire.

Vampires, whether live or dead, are generally born rather than made. However, a peasant from Strojineţi said that there is a class of female vampires which are really only half vampire; that is to say, they are not vampires by birth, but have been taught to be vampires by the real ones, and shown how to do things. They put enchantments on cows, take on the form of a girls' lover, and so kill her. They are helped by St. Andrew, so that the priest conceals from them the time that St. Andrew's Day comes. Such vampires are alive, but after they die they walk.

There is a character by which a live vampire can infallibly be distinguished. It is known that vampires fight with hemp brakes. Now if anyone comes to a house and asks for a hemp brake, say, "Come tomorrow for the stand and the H-axle of the hemp brake." The next day she will come. Then put three needles on the threshold with their points upwards and some bits of garlic. She will not be able to get out of the house until she gets out the needles and removes the garlic, so she will go to the door, and return and again go to the door, thus proving that she is a vampire (*strigoica*).

In general dead vampires come out every night except Saturday, when they are to be found in their graves. The vampires that are reanimated corpses or spirits of the dead disappear, like all evil spirits, at cockcrow. Vampires that are nothing else than witches or wizards can come out in the daytime all the year round, just like other human beings. Their power is greatest at new moon, and weakens as the moon grows old. The two periods in the course of the year when vampires are generally considered to be most active are St. Andrew's Eve and St. George's Eve. In Roşa, it is said that vampires begin to walk on St. Andrew's Eve, and separate after St. George's Day, after which they have no power, because flowers and the holy sweet basil begin to grow, and this shows that the power of God is increasing. This statement is interesting, as it shows that the peasant conceives of God as a god of fertility, and of vampires as inhabitants of the underworld. In Popeca, vampires are said to be at their worst before Easter. This would also bear out the idea of their being subdued by a rising God. In Mihalcea, they are said to walk only from St. Andrew's Eve to Epiphany. When the priest sings *Kyrie eleison* all evil spirits perish till next St. Andrew's Eve. In Siret they are said to be free from St. Andrew's Day till Transfiguration, and from St. George's Day till St. John's.

The precautions against visits from vampires are taken more especially before St. Andrew's Day and St. George's Day, but also before Easter Sunday and on the last day of the year. Garlic keeps off vampires, wolves, and evil spirits, and millet has a similar action. On St. Andrew's Eve and St. George's Eve, and before Easter and the New Year, windows should be anointed with garlic in the form of a cross, garlic put on the door and everything in the house, and all the cows in the cowshed should be rubbed with garlic. When vampires do enter, they enter by the chimney or by the keyhole, so these orifices call for special attention when garlic is being rubbed in. Even though the window is anointed with garlic, it is wisest to keep it shut. Especially on St. Andrew's Eve, all lamps may be put out and everything in the house never good to spin by moonlight, for vampires and *vârcolaci* get up to the sky by the thread turned upside down, so that if a vampire does come, it will not be able to ask any of the objects in the house to open the door. It is just as well for people not to sleep at all, but to tell stories right up to cockcrow. If you are telling stories, vampires cannot approach. Women should keep on saying their prayers. They may also beat on the hemp brakes to keep the vampires away. It is unwise to leave hemp brakes or shovels where vampires can get hold of them, for they like to ride on them. Vampires also like to take the tongues of hemp brakes as weapons and fight with them, till the sparks fly; hence the tongues should never be left fixed in the hemp brakes. Especially on St. George's Eve, it is a wise precaution to put on your shirt inside out, and to put a knife or scythe under your head when you sleep, turning the cutting edge outwards. It may also be as well to sleep with the feet where the head usually is, so that, if a vampire does enter, it will not find you.

At any time of the year it is well, especially at night-time, never to answer until anyone calls you three times, for vampires can ask a question twice but not three times. If you reply when they speak to you, they may turn your mouth skew, make you dumb, cut off your foot, or kill you.

There is a special kind of witch, *vidme*, who differs in her attributes from the witch that is called a vampire. The *vidme* are evil, bewitch people, and steal children. God said to them, "God will not help you in what you are doing." They replied, "And we will not help you to ascend." So God could not ascend to heaven. Elsewhere we are told that Christ reproved them, and they answered, "But you will not ascend where you thought you would, for we will cut your wings, so that you will remain down here." In a third variant, this discussion comes in connection with the Ascension. It is only after Christ has come to an understanding with these witches that he can ascend to heaven.

The following account of *vârcolaci*, considered to be the creatures which eat the sun and moon and thus cause eclipses, is taken from the Roumanian Academy's pamphlet *Credinţele Ţaranului Roman despre Cer*

63

și Stele (Beliefs of the Roumanian Peasant concerning the Sky and the Stars), by I. Otescu.

Vârcolaci are supposed to be different from any beings on the earth. They cause eclipses of the moon, and even of the sun, by mounting up to heaven and eating the moon or sun. Some think that they are animals smaller than dogs. Others that they are dogs, two in number. Others again think that they are dragons, or some kind of animal with many mouths, which suck like an octopus, others that they are spirits and can also be called *pricolici*. They have different origins; some say that they are the souls of unbaptised children, or of children of unmarried parents, cursed by God and turned into *vârcolaci*. Others say that they take rise if, when anyone is making maize porridge, they put the porridge stick into the fire, or if, when anyone is sweeping out the house at sunset, they sweep out the dust in the direction of the sun. Others again say that *vârcolaci* originate from the air of heaven, when women spin at night, especially at midnight, without a candle, especially if they cast spells with the thread they spin. Hence it is never good to spin by moonlight, for vampires and *vârcolaci* get up to the sky by the thread and eat the sun and moon. They fasten themselves to the thread, and the thread makes itself into a road for them. As long as the thread does not break the *vârcolaci* have power, and can go wherever they wish. They attack the heavenly bodies, they bite the moon, so that she appears covered with blood, or till none of her is left. But if the thread is broken their power is broken and they go to another part of the sky.

How is it that the moon comes out whole after an eclipse if it has been eaten up? Some people say that, as the moon is really stronger than the *vârcolaci*, they are just able to bite it, but in the end the moon conquers, for the world would come to an end if the moon were really eaten up.

G. F. Ciauşanu, in his *Superstitule poporului Román*, reports that in Vâlcea there are said to be beings who are called *vârcolaci*, because their spirit is *vârcolaci*. They are recognised by their pale faces and dry skin, and by the deep sleep into which they fall when they go to the moon to eat it. But they eat it only during an eclipse, and when the disc of the moon is red or copper coloured. The redness is the blood of the moon, escaping from the mouths of the vârcolaci and spreading over the moon.

When the spirit of the *vârcolac* wants to eat the moon, the man to whom the spirit belong begins to nod, falls into a deep sleep as if he had not slept for weeks, and remains as if dead. If he is roused or moved the sleep becomes eternal, for, when the spirit returns from its journey, it cannot find the mouth out of which it came, and so cannot go in.

During an eclipse the peasants in Vâlcea beat on fire shovels to frighten away the *vârcolaci* from the moon. In Puma they toll the church bells. Elsewhere they make noises with tongs, gridirons, and irons of all sorts, beat trays, and let off guns. Gipsies play on the fiddle and lute,—anything to make a noise.

Some people think that the *vârcolaci* pull at the moon and drop off when tired, others that the moon gets away very quickly from them, and they are just able to nip off a bit as she passes. The sun escapes, because the lion on which it rides fights with the *vârcolaci*. Some say that God orders the *vârcolaci* to eat the moon, so that men may repent and turn from evil.

It is curious that the word *vârcolac*, or *vrykolaka*, which is the general name for a vampire in Macedonia and Greece, is only exceptionally used to mean a vampire in Roumania, and usually means an animal which eats the moon. Vârcolac means "werewolf," and in Roumania it is the wolf or animal significance which predominates; in Macedonia, the human significance, the idea of devouring not being lost in either country.

A considerable number of vampire stories are of the type of Scott's William and Helen; the vampire comes to fetch his lady love, and takes her with him to his tomb.

In the first series of these stories, he loves one girl only, and seeks her out when she is alone; in the second series he chooses her out from other maidens at an evening gathering, and may destroy all other people present at the gathering.

The Girl and the Vampire.[4] (Story from Râmnic Sârat.) Once in a village there were a girl and a youth who were deeply in love, their parents did not know, and when the relations of the youth approached the parents of the girl with a proposal of marriage they were repulsed because the youth was poor. So the young man hanged himself on a tree, and became a vampire. As such he was able to come and visit the girl. But, although the girl had loved the man, she did not much like to have to do with an evil spirit. What could she do to escape from danger and sin? She went to a wise woman, and this wise woman advised her what to do. The vampire came one evening to make love to

---

[4] Ion Creanga 7 (1914): 82.

the girl and stayed late. When he knew that it was about time to leave, he said,—"Good night," and made ready to go. The girl, following the advice of the wise old woman, fixed into the back of his coat a needle, to which was attached one end of the thread from a large ball of thread. The vampire went away, and the ball unrolled and unrolled for some time and then, all at once, it stopped. The girl understood what had happened, and followed the clue given by the thread. She traced it along the road, and found that it entered into the churchyard, and went straight to a grave. There it entered the earth, and that was the end. She came home, but the next night, as twilight came on, she hastened to the churchyard, and stood some distance from the grave to see what would happen. It was not long before she saw the vampire coming out, going to another grave, opening it, eating the heart of the dead man buried there, and then setting out towards the village to visit her. She followed him as he left the churchyard. "Where were you this evening, and what did you see?" asked the vampire after he had greeted her. "Where was I? Nowhere, I saw nothing," said the girl. The vampire continued,—"I warn you that, if you do not tell me, your father will die." "Let him die, I know nothing, I've seen nothing, and I can say nothing." "Very well," said the vampire, and indeed in two days the girl's father was dead. He was buried with all due rites, and it was some time before the vampire again came to the girl.

One night, however, he came and made love to her as usual, but before leaving he said,-"Tell me where you were that evening, because, if you will not, your mother will die." "She may die nine times. How can I speak when I know nothing?" answered the girl.

After two days the mother died. She was duly buried. Again some time passed, and the vampire reappeared, and now he said,—"If you do not tell me what you saw that evening, you shall die too." "What if I do?" said she, "it will be no great loss. How can I invent a story, if I know nothing and have seen nothing?" "That is all very well, but what are you going to do now, for you are about to die?" replied the vampire.

On the advice of the wise old woman the girl called all her relations together and told them that she was going to die soon. When she was dead they were not to take her out by the door or by the window, but to break an opening in the walls of the house. They were not to bury her in the churchyard, but in the forest, and they were not to take her by the road but to go right across the fields until they came to a little hollow among the trees of the forest and here her grave was to be. And so it happened. The girl died, the wall of the house was broken down, and she was carried out on a bier across the fields to the margin of the forest.

After some time a wonderful flower, such as has never been seen, either before or after, grew up on her grave. One day the son of the emperor passed by and saw this flower, and immediately gave orders that it should be dug up well below the roots, brought to the castle, and put by his window. The flower flourished, and was more beautiful than ever, but the son of the emperor pined. He himself did not know what was the matter, he could neither eat nor drink. What was the matter? At night the flower became again the maiden, as beautiful as before. She entered in at the window, and passed the night with the emperor's son without his knowing it. However, one night she could contain herself no longer, and kissed him, and he awoke and saw her. After that, they pledged troth to each other, they told the emperor and empress, they were married, and they lived very happily together. There was only one drawback to their happiness. The wife would never go out of the house. She was afraid of the vampire.

One day, however, her husband took her with him in a carriage to go to church, when there, at a corner, who should there be but the vampire. She jumped out of the carriage and rushed to the church. She ran, the vampire ran, and just had his hand on her as they both reached the church together. She hid behind a holy picture. The vampire stretched out his hand to seize her, when all at once the holy picture fell on his head, and he disappeared in smoke. And the wife lived with the emperor's son free from all danger and sin for the rest of her life.

A variant of this story is given by Manas'ev in his *Russian Popular Tales*, and is quoted by Ralston in his *Russian Folk Tales*. The main points of difference between the Russian and the Roumanian story are that, in the Russian tale the following occurs:

1. The first meeting of the lover and the girl was at an evening gathering on St Andrew's Eve.
2. He asked the girl to see him on his way home, and proposed marriage to her.
3. The girl's mother advised fastening the thread to his coat; the next night she fastened it to him, followed him to the churchyard, and saw him eating the dead. He is, however, live, not dead.

4. They met again at the gathering. Questions, answers, the death of the girl's parents and herself, and the digging of the flower by the emperor's son are imilar in both versions. The girl makes it a condition of marriage that she does not go to church for four years.

5. Going to church earlier, she sees the lover at the window, still refuses to answer, and her husband and son die.

6. The grandmother gives her holy water and water of life. The lover again asks his question. The girl tells him that she saw him eating corpses, and then, by sprinkling water on him, turns him into ashes. With the water of life, she brings back to life her husband and son.

Vampire Story from Botoşani.[5] A girl and a young man were once in love, but the youth died and became a vampire. The girl knew nothing of this. She happened to be alone in her parents' house, and she put out all the lights and went to bed as usual. Now vampires can enter into empty houses or into unclean houses, but the girl's house was clean and holy, so he could not come in. Instead of coming in he called at the window, speaking in the same tone and using the same words as he did when alive. "Stupid girl, come with me," he said, and took her hand and led her, undressed as she was, to his tomb. "Go in," he said. "No, friend, I'm afraid," she said. He went in first, and called, "Come quicker." "Wait," she said, "I've lost my beads. They must have fallen hereabouts." And she ran

---

5 *Ibid.*, 5 (1912): 11.

and ran until she saw a house with a light. She went in and found a dead man called Avram on a bench. She drew the bolts of the door and lay down in hiding behind the oven. The vampire came after her with true vampire persistency. He knocked at the window, saying, "Avram, open the door." Avram was himself a vampire, and was going to obey and open the door. But the hen saw what was happening, and said to the cock,—"Crow, so as to save the poor girl." "No, you crow. It is not my turn." So the hen crowed quickly before Avram could get to the door, and the girl escaped, because she was clean and holy, and vampires do not easily get hold of clean souls.

In a variant of this story the vampire comes to his sweetheart, and takes her away with him to his grave. She is able, however, to escape by stopping up the entrance to the grave with woven linen, and running away. It has been suggested that the idea behind the stopping of the path of the vampire with linen is the same as that when millet seed is put in his way; he is obliged to disentangle and straighten out the threads of the linen in the one case, or count the millet seed in the other.

A simpler variant, in which the hero is a dragon (*zmeu*) and not a vampire, is as follows:—A soldier relates how a dragon in the form of a tongue of fire entered into a woman's house by either the door or the window. It became a man, made love to her, and then again became a flame and disappeared. As the hero is a *zmeu* and not a vampire, the "grave" motive is wanting.

In the following lover stories, the action begins in a crowded evening gathering:

A Story from Botoșani.[6] There was once a time when vampires were as common as leaves of grass, or berries in a pail, and they never kept still, but wandered round at night among the people. They walked about and joined the evening gatherings in the villages, and, when there were many young people together, the vampires could carry out their habit of inspiring fear, and sucking human blood like leeches. Once, when an evening gathering was in full swing, in came an uninvited guest, the vampire. But no one knew that he was a vampire. He was in the form of a handsome youth, full of fun. He said "Good day" very politely, sat down on a bank beside the girls, and began to talk, and all the girls imagined that he was a youth from another part of the village. Then the vampire began to tell stories and jokes, so that the girls did not know what to do for laughter. He played and jested and bandied words with them without ceasing. But there was one girl to whom he paid special attention, and teased unmercifully. "Keep still, friend. Have I done anything to annoy you?" said she. But he still kept on pinching her, till she was black and blue. "What is it, friend? You go too far with your joke. Do you want to make an end of me?" said the poor girl. At the moment her distaff fell. When she stooped to pick it up, what did she see? The tail of the vampire. Then she said to the girl next to her,—"Let's go. Run away. The creature is a vampire." The other girl was laughing so much that she did not understand. So the girl who knew the dreadful secret went out alone into the yard, on the pretext that she had to take some lengths of woven linen to the attic. Frightened out of her wits, she

---

[6] *Ibid.*, 4 (1911): 202.

ran away with the linen, she ran into a forest, old as the world and black as her fear.

Her companions at the gathering awaited her return. They looked and waited until they saw that she was not coming back. Where could she be? "You must fetch her wherever she is," roared the vampire, with bloodshot eyes and hair standing on end. As the girl could not be found, the vampire killed all the rest of the merrymakers. He sucked their blood, he threw their flesh and bones under the bed, cut off their lips, and put their heads in a row in the window. They looked as if they were laughing. He strung up their intestines on a nail, saying they were strings of beads, and then he fled away. He arrived at the forest where the girl had taken refuge, and found her under a beech-tree. "Why did you come here, little girl? Why did you run away from the gathering?" The girl, poor thing, was so frightened that her tongue clove to her mouth, and she could say nothing. "You are afraid, little girl. Come home with me. You will feel better there." Then, involuntarily, she asked,—"Where?" "Here in the forest. Come quicker," said the vampire.

They arrived at a hole in the depth of the forest, and she saw that this was the home of the vampire. He pressed her to enter first. "No, no. I don't want to. You go first." So the vampire went in, and began to sweep and clear up. The girl, however, stopped up the hole with the lengths of linen, and fled quickly towards the east. In her flight she saw a little light a long way off. She ran towards the light, came to a house, and found it empty, except for a dead man, who was lying stretched out on a table, with a torch at his head, and his hands crossed on his breast. What was she to do? She entered the house, climbed up on to the stove, and went to sleep, worn out by suffering and fear. And she would have rested well, had not the terrible vampire pursued her. He had thrown aside the linen, and rushed after her, mad with rage. He came into the house, and the dead man rose, and they fought and wrestled till the cock crew and the girl awoke. Now the light was out, the dead man was gone, and the only sound was the song of the little cricket. The girl was left alone with her guardian angel. The dead man and the vampire both vanished at cockcrow, for both were vampires. Waking up in the darkness, the girl looked round the house three times, thought she was at home and had had a horrible dream, and then fell asleep again calmly and fearlessly. When she woke again, and saw all the beauties of the forest, and heard all the songs of the birds, she was amazed and thought herself in heaven. She did not stop long in wonder, but set out for her parents' house, hoping to bring them back with her.

She reached her home, and began to tell about the vampire and how he had gone, and what beautiful things she had seen in the woods of paradise. The parents looked at her, and, full of amazement and doubt, made the sign of the cross. The girl sank into the ground, deeper and deeper, for she too had become a vampire, poor thing. The vampire had bewitched her, and the beauty of the dwelling in the wood had enchanted her too much.

Another variant of the story[7] is as follows:

---

[7] *Ibid.*, 6 (1913): 237.

There was an evening gathering in the village, as is the custom. But the youths and maidens present were not the children of well-to-do peasants. The gathering was held in a deserted house; the youths were a noisy, laughing, mocking crowd who made themselves heard from one end of the village to the other, and the girls were just like them. They made a great fire, the girls started spinning, the boys told all kinds of jokes, and the girls shook with laughter. After it had grown late, three young men, unknown to the company, entered the house. "Good evening, good evening," was said, and they joined in the general conversation. While everyone was talking, one of the girls dropped her distaff. The distaff fell under the strangers' feet, and the girl stooped to pick it up. When she went back to her seat she was as white as chalk. "What is it?" asked one of those near her. And the girl murmured that the three strangers had horses' hooves instead of feet. What was to be done? They whispered to one another, and to the boys, that the three strangers were vampires, not men. Then one by one, one by one, they slipped out of the door, and wended their ways homewards. The three vampires remained as vampires, but they did not remain alone in the house, for there was a girl asleep on the oven.

With the dawn of the next day, the sister of the sleeping girl, together with some friends, came to see what had happened to her. When they were still some distance from the house they saw a grinning face looking out of the window—"Oh, oh," they said, "our sister is laughing." They drew nearer, and, entering into the house, were horror-struck and made the sign of the cross. It was the head only which was in the window; the lips were cut off, and so the face seemed to smile. Her intestines were stretched out on the nails and on shelves, and the whole house was stained with blood. Poor girl![8]

In the two following vampire stories from Siret, vampires are thought of as wizard like beings, being men or women capable of projecting their soul from their body at will:

A woman from Siret[9] tells the following:—Vampires are just like other folk, only that God has ordained that they should wander over the country and kill people. There was one that wandered through ten villages, killing their inhabitants. He had a little house in the plain, which was always empty except when he himself was there. One day he thought of going on a journey, and baked bread in preparation. He made ten loaves and put them on the table. Twelve men who were going to work passed the cottage, and noticed that there was a light. One of the men said,—"I'll just go in and light my pipe." They all entered, and the vampire became a cat. The men saw that there was no human being in the house, so they took all the loaves, except one, which they left because they had seen the cat. This was lucky for them, for otherwise they would all have been bewitched and died.

The vampire went round the villages, taking with him the one loaf.

---

[8] This delightful habit of cutting off the lips of their victims is not peculiar to vampires. It is the way Montenegrins, Turks, and others occasionally treat their defeated enemies.

[9] *Ion Creanga* 6 (1913): 80.

When the men returned from work, they again passed the cottage and again saw a light. They entered, and this time saw the vampire, who told them of their escape. Their luck was great, for in all the villages where the vampire had wandered he had killed men and torn them to bits.

Vampire Story from Siret.[10] An old man with some soldiers was driving in a cart in Transilvania, trying to find where he could get some hay. Night came on during their journey, so they stopped at a lonely house in a plain. The woman of the house received them, put maize porridge (*mămăligă*) and milk on the table for them, and then went away. The soldiers ate the maize porridge, and after their meal looked for the old woman to thank her, but were unable to find her. Climbing up to the attic to see if she was there, they found seven bodies lying down, one of which was the woman's. They were frightened and fled, and, as they looked back, they saw seven little lights descending on the house. These were the souls of the vampires. Had the soldiers turned the bodies with their faces downwards, the souls would never have been able to enter the bodies again.

In the following stories vampires are witches (in one case a wizard) pure and simple. In the first two we have them joining in witches' revels; in the others they get hold of the "power" of cows for their own ends:

There was a lady of the highest society in Botoşani who was dressed up in beautiful Paris clothes for a party on

---

[10] *Ibid.,*17.

Dec. 31st; she went into her nursery, got out by the chimney, and came back all in rags, and exhausted.[11]

A lad who was in service with a female vampire noticed once that she was covered with blood during the day-time. He watched her closely, and saw that she anointed herself with something, and went out by the chimney. The lad also anointed himself with the ointment in the box, and went out of the chimney after his mistress. He arrived at a far off desert region, where the vampires fought. He watched them stabbing one another and fighting. The vampires go with their bodies, not their souls only. The ointment with which the vampires anoint themselves is made of the grease of serpents, hedgehogs, and badgers.[12]

One or the main characters of the live (witchlike) vampires is that they can take the "power" of cows.

There was once a female vampire (*strigoica*) who had no cow of her own. However, she kept a wooden cow in her attic, and milked it day and night continually. She had taken all the milk of other people's cows, and brought it to her own wooden cow.[13]

A woman who was a vampire (*strigoica*) went to confession and told the priest that she had taken the "power" of other people's cows (*i.e.* got more milk from her own cow at their expense). The priest said to her ,—"Take the butter from this milk, go into the forest, anoint a tree with it, and then, after three days, go back and see what happens." She did this

---

[11] *Ibid.*, 7 (1914): 24.
[12] *Ibid.*, 6 (1913): 306.
[13] *Ibid.*, 18.

and found a great number of serpents and other horrible creatures in the butter. "You must know," said the priest, "that these will suck your blood in the next world, because you have taken "power" from everything in this world."[14]

In the variant given below, the woman is not called a vampire, but just a *baba* or old wife:

An old woman in Strojineţi got as much milk from her cow as one usually gets from ten cows. A poor woman, who was getting very little milk from her cow, asked the old wife to cure it. The old wife took butter from her cow, and butter from the poor woman's cow, and put both lots into water. In the old wife's butter there were numbers of serpents, lizards, worms, and other horrible creatures; in that of the woman, there were only little fishes. "Look," said the old wife. "In the other world these serpents will suck from me. If you wish to share my fate I will arrange that your cow shall give much milk also." But the poor woman did not wish this. When the old wife died, a light was seen from time to time going to her house. It was seen chiefly by rather dull people.[15]

In the following story we have a contest of strength between a witch and a vampire, two beings that seem of exactly the same nature, the witch being the more admirable only in that she takes the side of the human beings.

The Witch versus the Vampire.[16] A lady in Siret had a cow, and a vampire had taken away its "power." But she found a

---

[14] *Ibid.*, 105.
[15] Ibid., 108.
[16] *Ibid.*, 18.

wise woman, named Hartopaniţa, who knew how to break the power of the vampire. She saw him once in the house. She made a sign with her finger, screwed up her mouth, and said a word which bound the vampire to the spot. He remained as if frozen, and could not move a step. But he caused the wise woman to come out in sores, and she could not get rid of them till she had asked him to forgive her.

In the following three accounts the vampire has the character of a devil, and the word *strigoi* could be replaced by *drac*:

Vampires wander at the cross-roads. If anyone has a great wish, and is entirely fearless, there is the means to attain the wish. Go to the cross-roads at night. Take a large vessel with water. Make a fire, and, when the water boils, take a black cat, without one white hair, and drop her into the pot. A black cat is supposed to represent the soul of the devil. After it is quite dark, when the pot with the cat in it is boiling vigorously, devils begin to come to ask you to stop boiling the cat. You must not speak a word. You must wait until the chief of all the devils comes, for he will come last of all. He will ask you to stop boiling the cat, just as the other devils did; but he will also promise you everything you wish. Then you will let him take the cat, and in exchange you will receive whatever you most desire.[17]

The next two stories are about the danger of sneezing.

---

[17] *Ibid.*, 5 (1912): 244.

The Thief and the Vampire.[18] There were once two part-
ners, a thief and a vampire. "'Where are you going this
evening?" said the thief to the vampire. "I am going to bewitch the son of Ion," said the vampire. "Don't go there. It
is there that I want to go this evening to steal oxen. You
can go somewhere else." "Go somewhere else yourself,"
said the vampire. "Why should you go to Ion's house of all
places? He has only one son, and there are heaps of other
houses you could go to," said the thief. "No, I'm going to
Ion's," said the vampire. "Well, I'm going there too," said
the thief. Both of them went. The vampire went to the
door, and the thief to the window. Ion's son inside
sneezed, and the thief said quickly,—"Long life." This
took away the vampire's power. He was able to make the
boy's nose bleed, but he did not die. The thief then went
in and told the parents what had happened, and they gave
him some oxen as a reward. It is always well to say "Long
life" when anyone sneezes.

Sneezing.[19] A young noble was about to start on a journey
and his horse was waiting saddled and bridled. There was
a thief creeping up to steal the horse. As he came near he
saw a vampire just under the window, waiting for an op-
portunity to put a spell on the noble. The noble sneezed,
and quickly the thief said,—"Good health," for if he had
not done so the vampire would have seized the occasion to
bewitch the noble, and he would have died. It was, however, the vampire who burst with anger at missing his
chance. People came out to see what was the matter. The
thief showed them the burst body of the vampire, and ex-

---

[18] *Ibid.,* 6 (1913): 51.
[19] *Ibid.*

plained what had happened. The parents were so glad that their son had escaped that they gave the horse to the thief as a reward. This shows us that we must always say "Good health" when anyone sneezes.

It is clear that the idea behind the word *strigoi* varies from one account to another. While the word *strigoi* generally denotes a reanimated corpse like the *vrykolaka* of Greece and Macedonia, its use to denote a witch or wizard who can project body or soul is common in Roumania, and especially in Moldavia. Its significance has become less terrible. Witches in Roumania are often little more than wise old women, or *babas*, who in their turn are only less common than leaves of grass; they also attempt good deeds as well as evil.

[*Folklore* 37, pp.320-349, 1926]

Printed in the USA
CPSIA information can be obtained
at www.ICGtesting.com
LVHW040335300923
759610LV00003B/613